John Adams

The Wound-Dresser

for Baritone Voice and Piano Reduction

Vocal Score

Archive Edition

HENDON MUSIC

AN IMAGEM COMPANY

DISTRIBUTED BY

7777 W. BLUEMOUND RD. P.O. BOX 13819 MILWAUKEE, WI 53213

www.boosey.com
www.halleonard.com

Published by Hendon Music, Inc.
a Boosey & Hawkes company
229 West 28th Street, 11th Floor
New York   NY 10001

www.boosey.com

Commissioned by Carillon Importers on behalf of Absolut Vodka with assistance from the Saint Paul Chamber Orchestra through a gift from Daniel and Constance Kunin.

First Performed February 24, 1989, at Ordway Music Theater in St. Paul, Minnesota, by Sanford Sylvan, baritone, and the Saint Paul Chamber Orchestra, conducted by John Adams.

Recorded by Sanford Sylvan, baritone, and the Orchestra of St. Lukes, conducted by John Adams, on Nonesuch 79218.

Bearing the bandages, water and sponge,
Straight and swift to my wounded I go,
Where they lie on the ground after the battle brought in,
Where their priceless blood reddens the grass the ground,
Or to the rows of the hospital tent, or under the roof 'd hospital,
To the long rows of cots up and down each side I return,
To each and all one after another I draw near, not one do I miss,
An attendant follows holding a tray, he carries a refuse pail,
Soon to be filled with clotted rags and blood, emptied, and filled again.

I onward go, I stop,
With hinged knees, and steady hand to dress wounds,
I am firm with each, the pangs are sharp yet unavoidable,
One turns to me his appealing eyes—poor boy! I never knew you,
Yet I think I could not refuse this moment to die for you, if that would save
    you.

On, on I go, (open doors of time! open hospital doors!)
The crushed head I dress, (poor crazed hand tear not the bandage away,)
The neck of the cavalry-man with the bullet through and through I examine,
Hard the breathing rattles, quite glazed already the eye, yet life struggles
    hard,

(Come sweet death! be persuaded O beautiful death!
In mercy come quickly.)
From the stump of the arm, the amputated hand,
I undo the clotted lint, remove the slough, wash off the matter and blood,
Back on his pillow the soldier bends with curv'd neck and side-falling head,
His eyes are closed, his face is pale, he dares not look on the bloody stump,
And has not yet look'd on it.

I dress a wound in the side, deep, deep,
But a day or two more, for see the frame all wasted and sinking,
And the yellow-blue countenance see.
I dress the perforated shoulder, the foot with the bullet-wound,
Cleanse the one with a gnawing and putrid gangrene, so sickening, so
    offensive,
While the attendant stands behind aside me holding the tray and pail.

I am faithful, I do not give out,
The fractured thigh, the knee, the wound in the abdomen,
These and more I dress with impassive hand, (yet deep in my breast a fire,
    a burning flame.)

Thus in silence in dreams' projections,
Returning, resuming, I thread my way through the hospitals,
The hurt and the wounded I pacify with soothing hand,
I sit by the restless all the dark night, some are so young,
Some suffer so much, I recall the experience sweet and sad,
(Many a soldier's loving arms about this neck have cross'd and rested,
Many a soldier's kiss dwells on these bearded lips.)

NOTE BY THE COMPOSER

Walt Whitman spent the better part of the Civil War years in Washington, D.C., living in a series of small, unfurnished rooms, all the time supported by the meager salary of a federal clerkship. His sole, consuming passion was his self-appointed task of ministering to the tens of thousands of sick and maimed soldiers who crowded the hospitals in the surrounding area, many of them little more than unheated and unventilated canvas tents hurriedly constructed by the unprepared Army of the Potomac. Virtually every day, barring his own illness or ever-increasing exhaustion, Whitman rose early and went to the hospitals, going from ward to ward to visit with the sick and wounded young men. For those who were unable to do so, he wrote letters home. For others he provided small gifts of fruit, candy or tobacco. He dressed the wounds of the maimed and the amputees and often sat up throughout the night with the most agonizing cases, almost all of whom he knew on a first-name basis. It was surely no poetic exaggeration when he later said that during these years many a young soldier had died in his, Walt Whitman's, arms.

Because the scope of his work is so grand and inclusive, and because he yearned throughout his life to embrace the entire universe in his poems, it has been tempting for succeeding generations to appropriate Whitman for any number of causes or points of view. For instance, one would easily assume the poet's sentiments to be fervently anti-war. In fact this was not the case, as the poems in *Drum-Taps* reveal. This slim volume, the only literary work he allowed himself to compose during the war years, is remarkably honest in that it expresses not just the horror and degradation of war, but also the thrill of battle and the almost manic exhilaration of one caught up in a righteous cause. Whitman hated war—this particular war and all wars—but he was no pacifist. Like his idol, Lincoln, he never ceased to believe in the Union's cause and in the dreadful necessity of victory.

The Wound-Dresser is a setting for baritone voice and orchestra of a fragment from the poem of the same name. As always with Whitman, it is in the first person, and it is the most intimate, most graphic and most profoundly affecting evocation of the act of nursing the sick and the dying that I know of. It is also astonishingly free of any kind of hyperbole or amplified emotion, yet the detail of the imagery is of a precision that could only be attained by one who had been there.

The Wound-Dresser is not just about the Civil War; nor is it just about young men dying (although it is locally about both). It strikes me as a statement about human compassion of the kind that is acted out on a daily basis, quietly and unobtrusively and unselfishly and unfailingly. Another poem in the same volume states its them in other words: "Those who love each other shall become invincible..."

—JOHN ADAMS
December 22, 1988

Duration: ca. 20 minutes

PIANO VOCAL SCORE

THE WOUND-DRESSER

JOHN ADAMS

REV 4/89

BEAR-ING___ THE BAN-DAG-ES,

WA-TER___ AND SPONGE,   STRAIGHT AND SWIFT___ TO MY WOUND-ED   I

GO.   WHERE THEY LIE___ON THE GROUND___ AF-TER THE BAT-TLE___ BROUGHT

IN,   WHERE THEIR PRICE-LESS BLOOD   RED-DENS THE

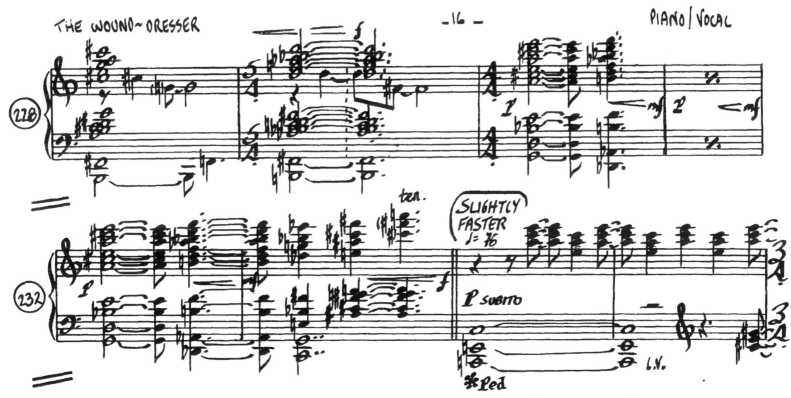

WHILE THE AT-

TEN-DANT STANDS BE-HIND A-SIDE ME HOLD-ING THE TRAY AND PAIL,

THESE AND MORE   I   DRESS   WITH IM- PAS - SIVE   HAND,___   (YET

DEEP   IN MY BREAST,   A   FIRE   A   BURN-ING FLAME.)

DWELLS   ON THESE BEARD-ED   LIPS. ____